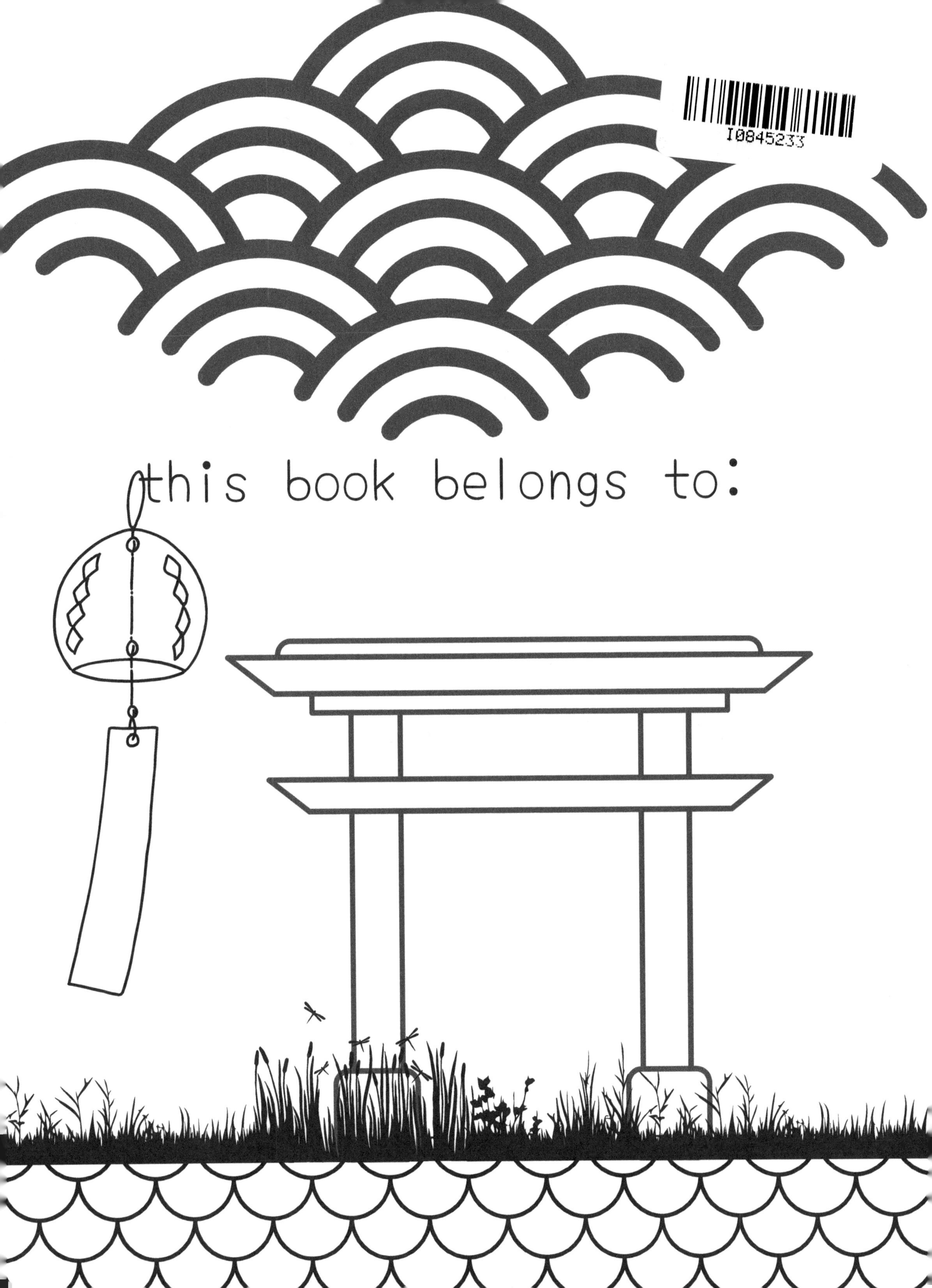
this book belongs to:

人生に美を見つけることが、豊かな心を持つ秘訣です。

Finding beauty in life is the
secret to having a rich heart.

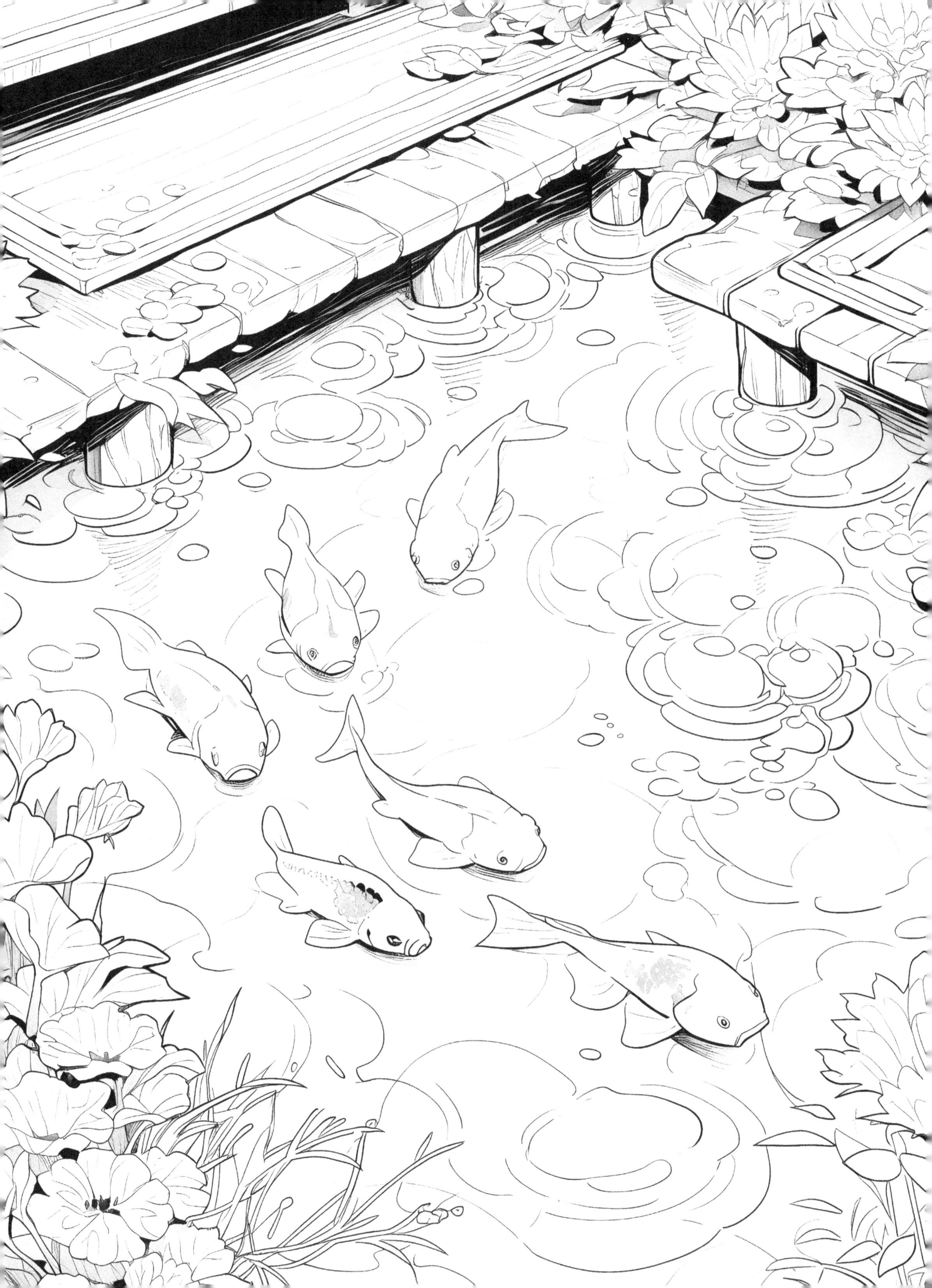

京都の古都、歴史の語り部

Kyoto, the ancient capital, a
storyteller of history.

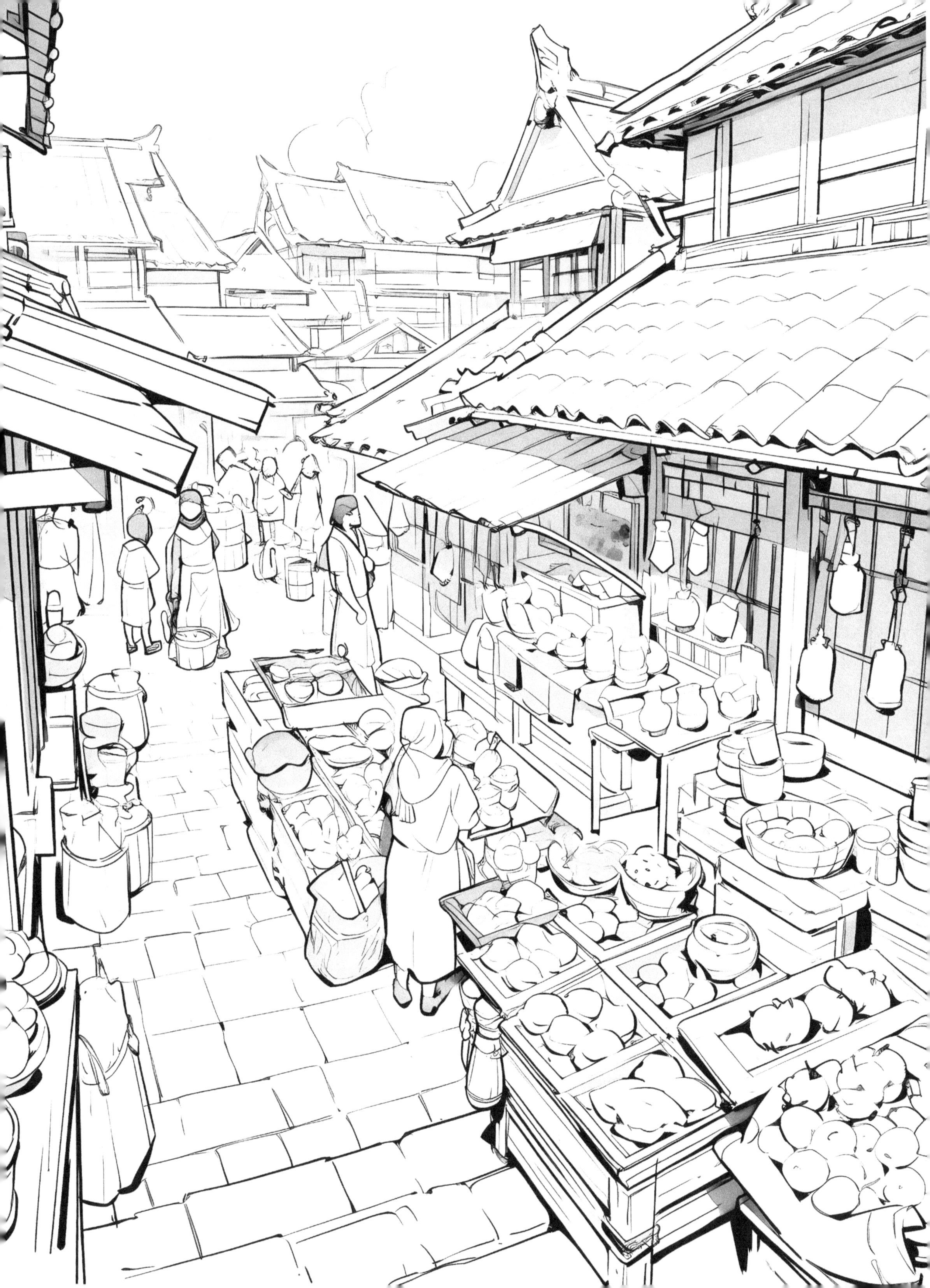

風のささやき、心の平穏

The whispers of the wind bring peace
to the heart.

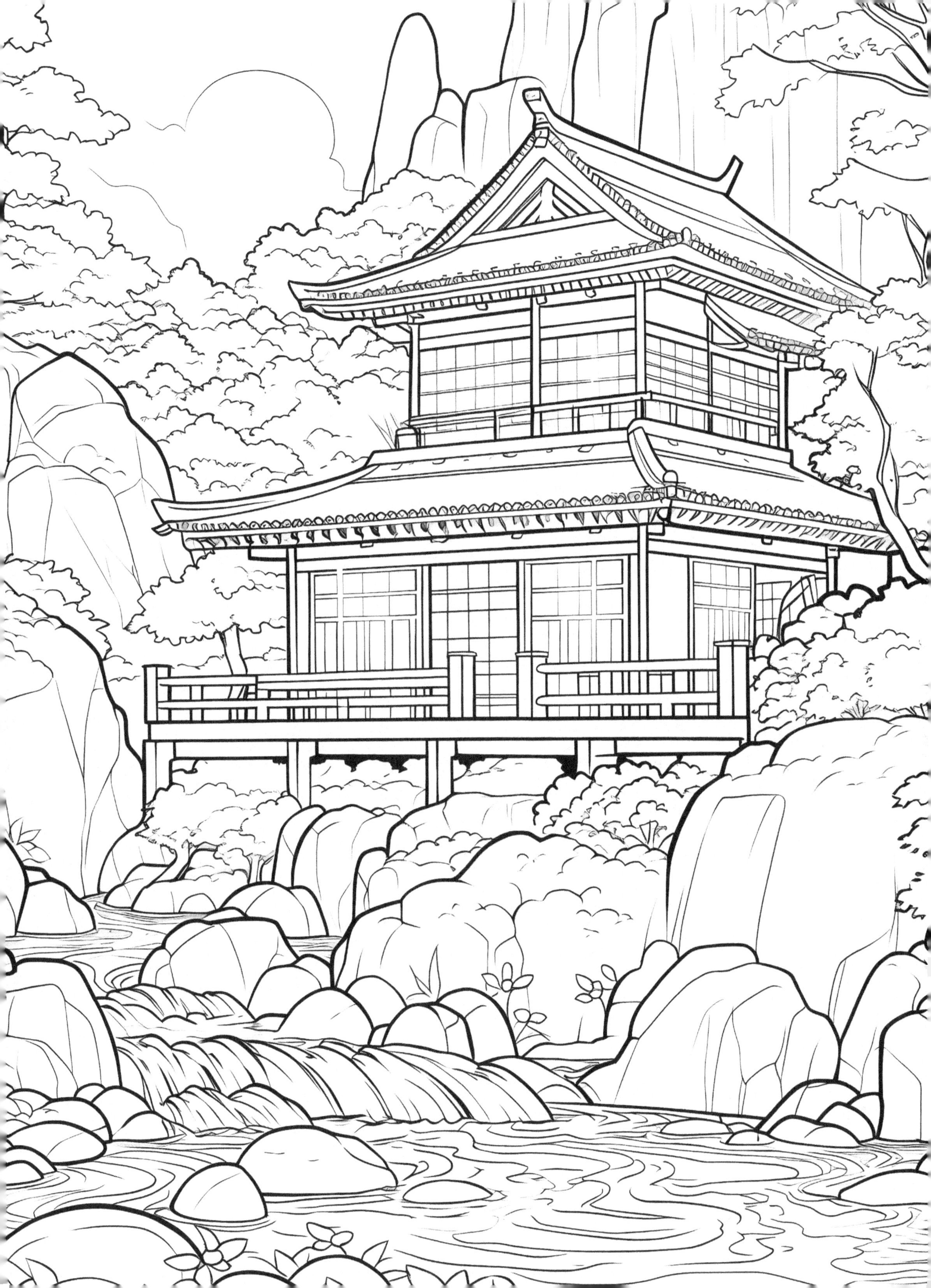

着物の風雅、美の華

The elegance of kimono, the flower of beauty.

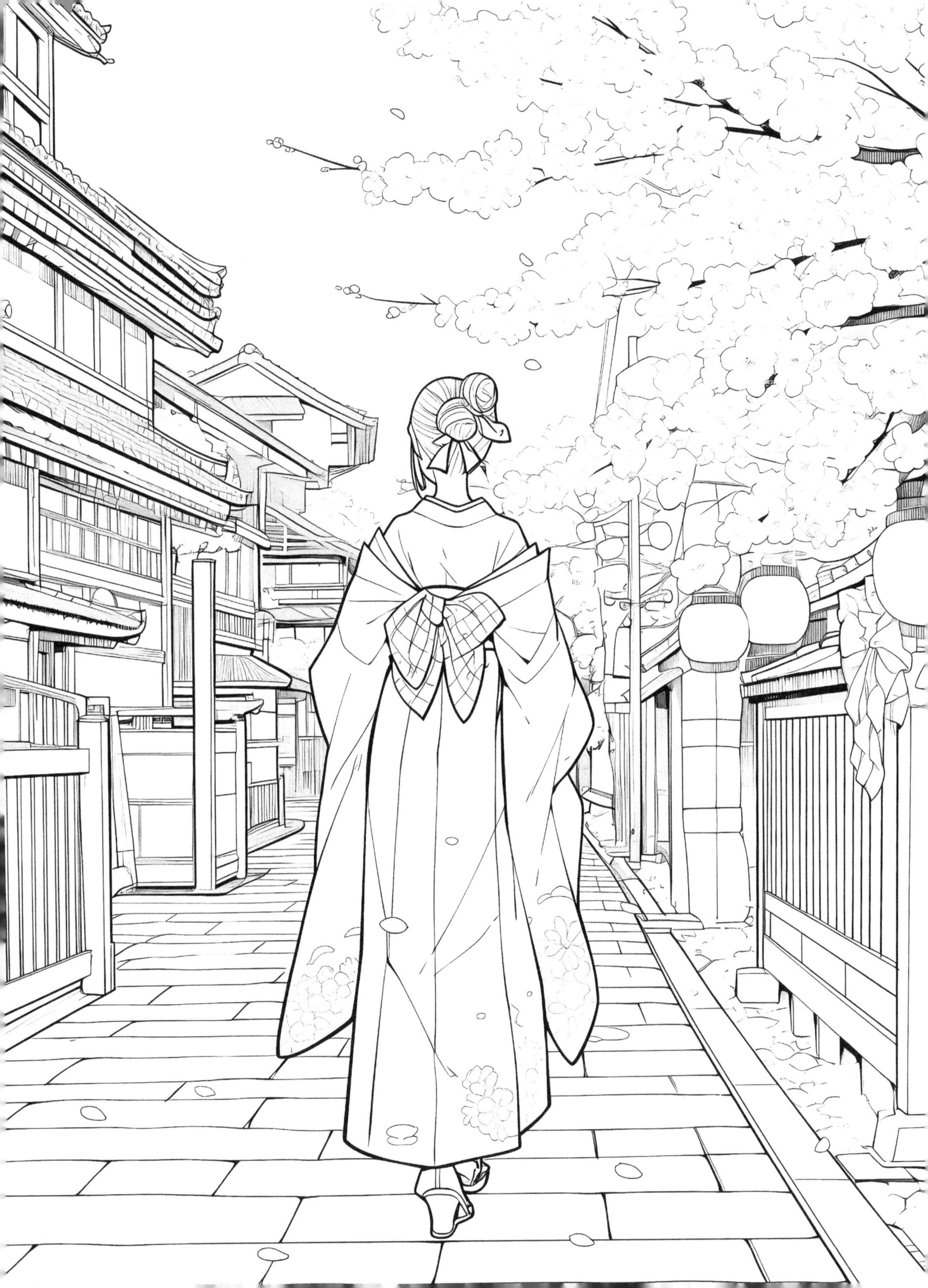

山水画のような風景、絵筆で描く

Scenery like a landscape
painting, painted with a brush.

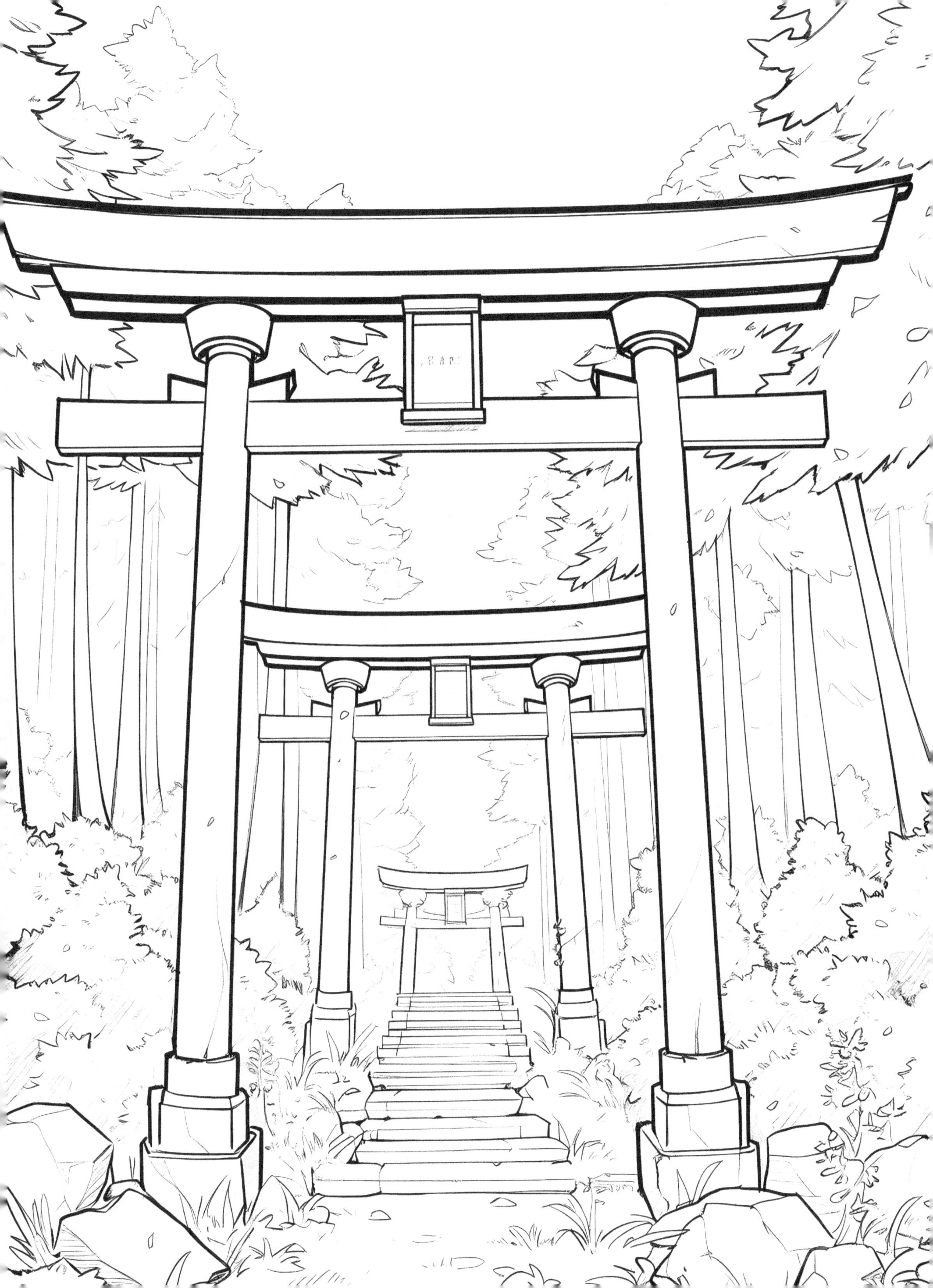

土俵に立つ者は一心同体

Those who stand on the dohyo are of
one mind and body.

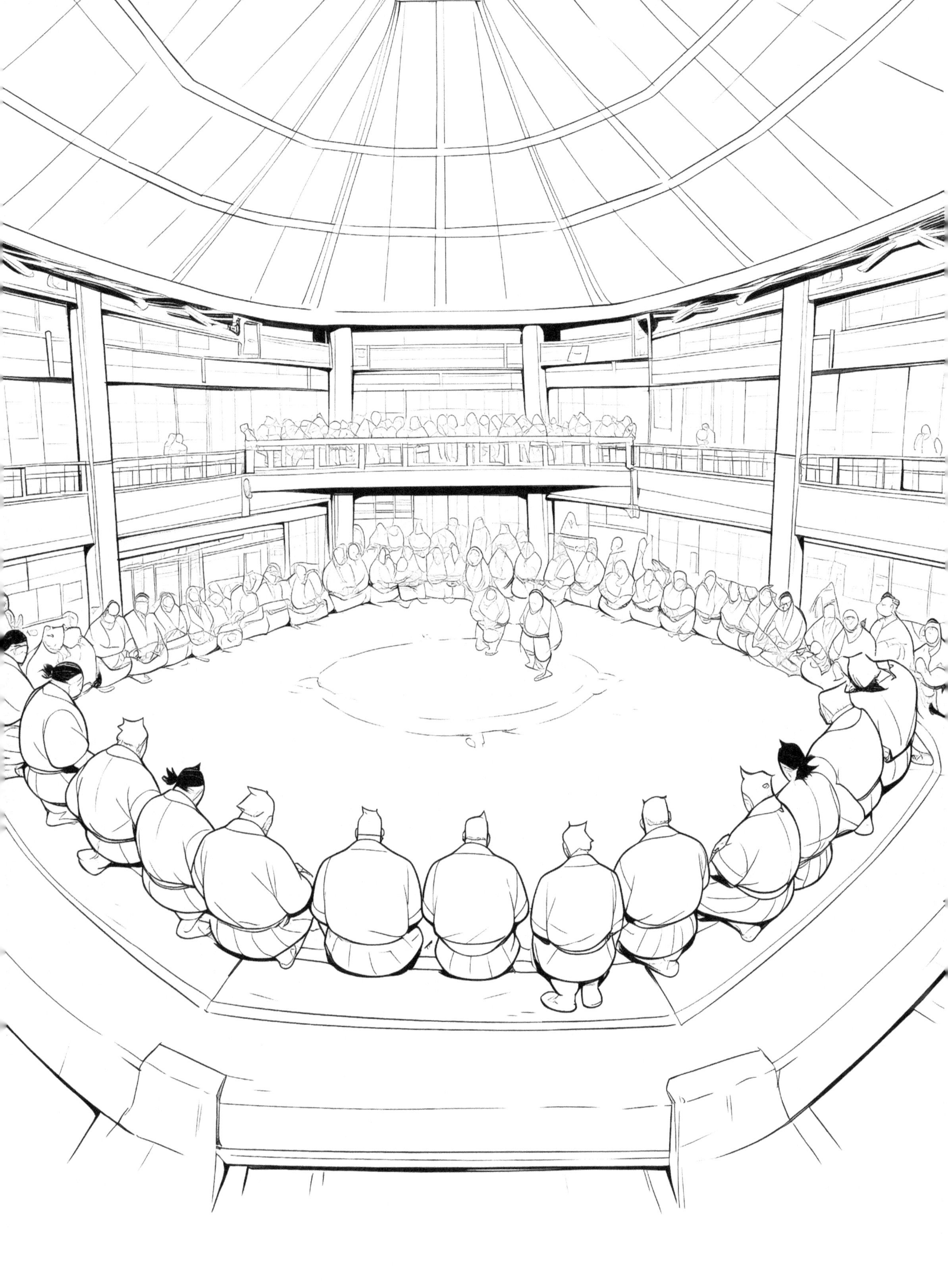

誇り高き浪人、道を求める旅人

The proud ronin, a
traveler seeking the path.

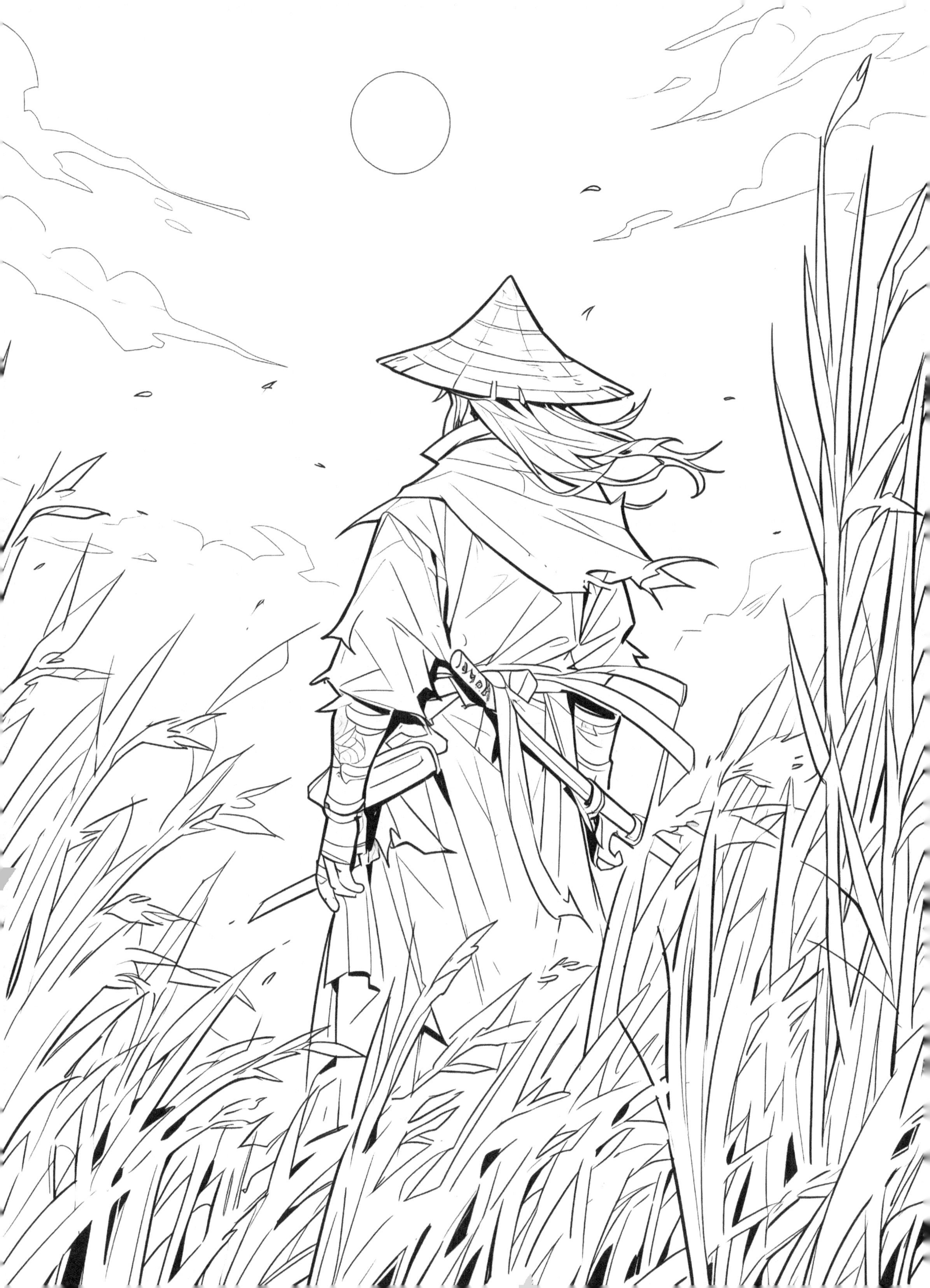

茶道の心、一期一会

The spirit of tea ceremony, each
encounter is unique.

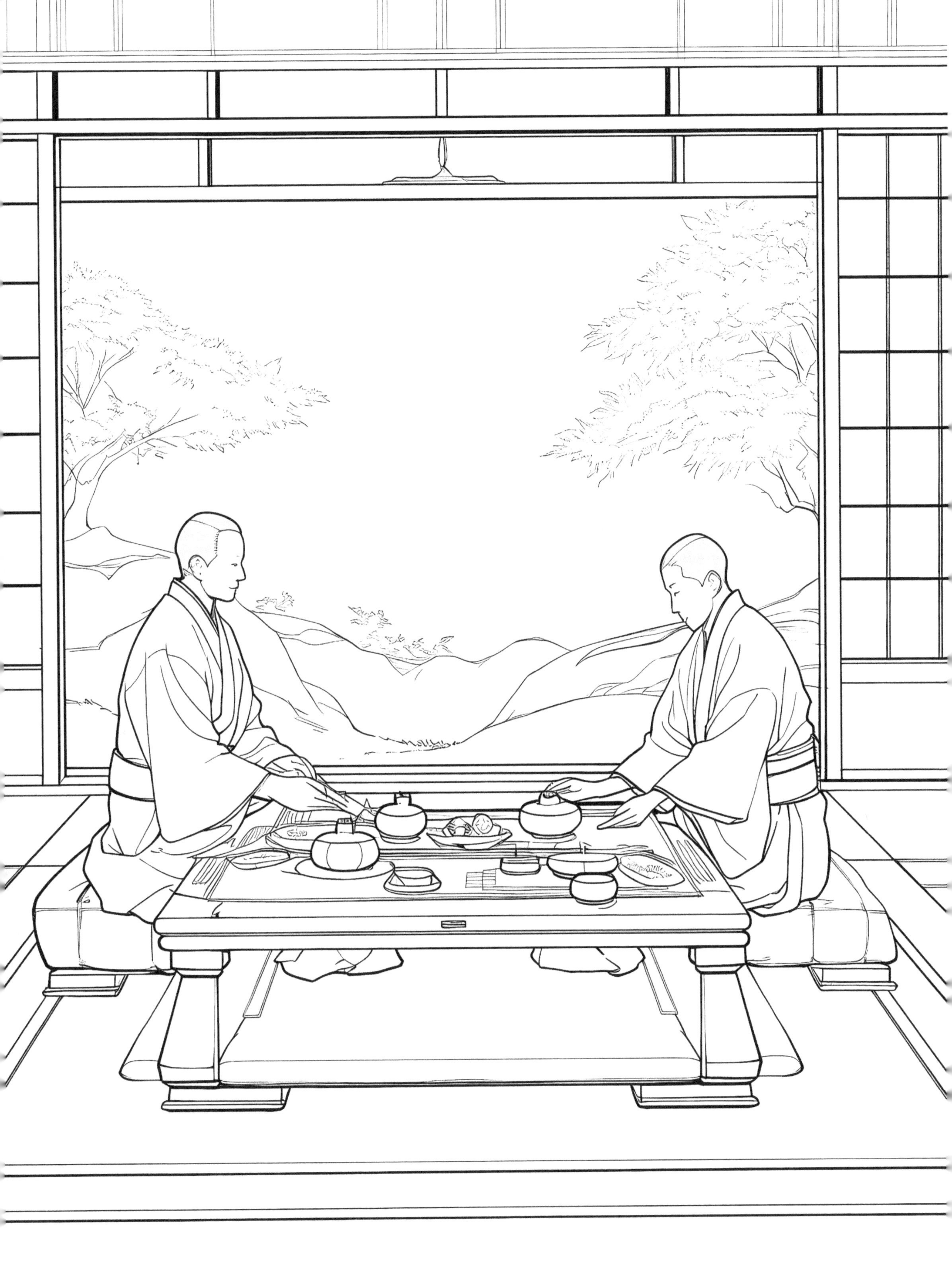

謙虚な心は美しさの源

A humble heart is the source of beauty.

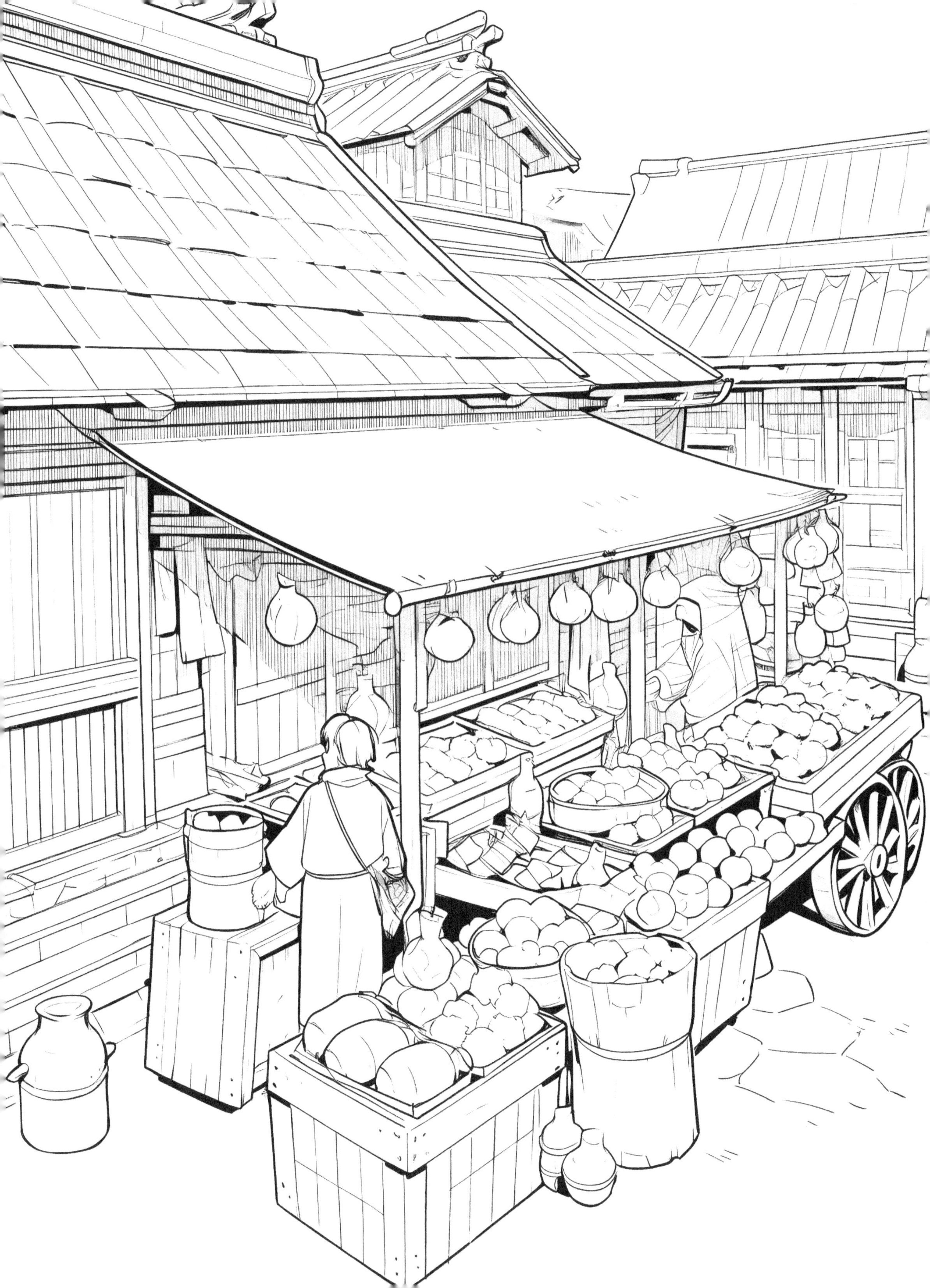

門をくぐれば、新たなる世界が広がる

Passing through the gate, a new world
expands

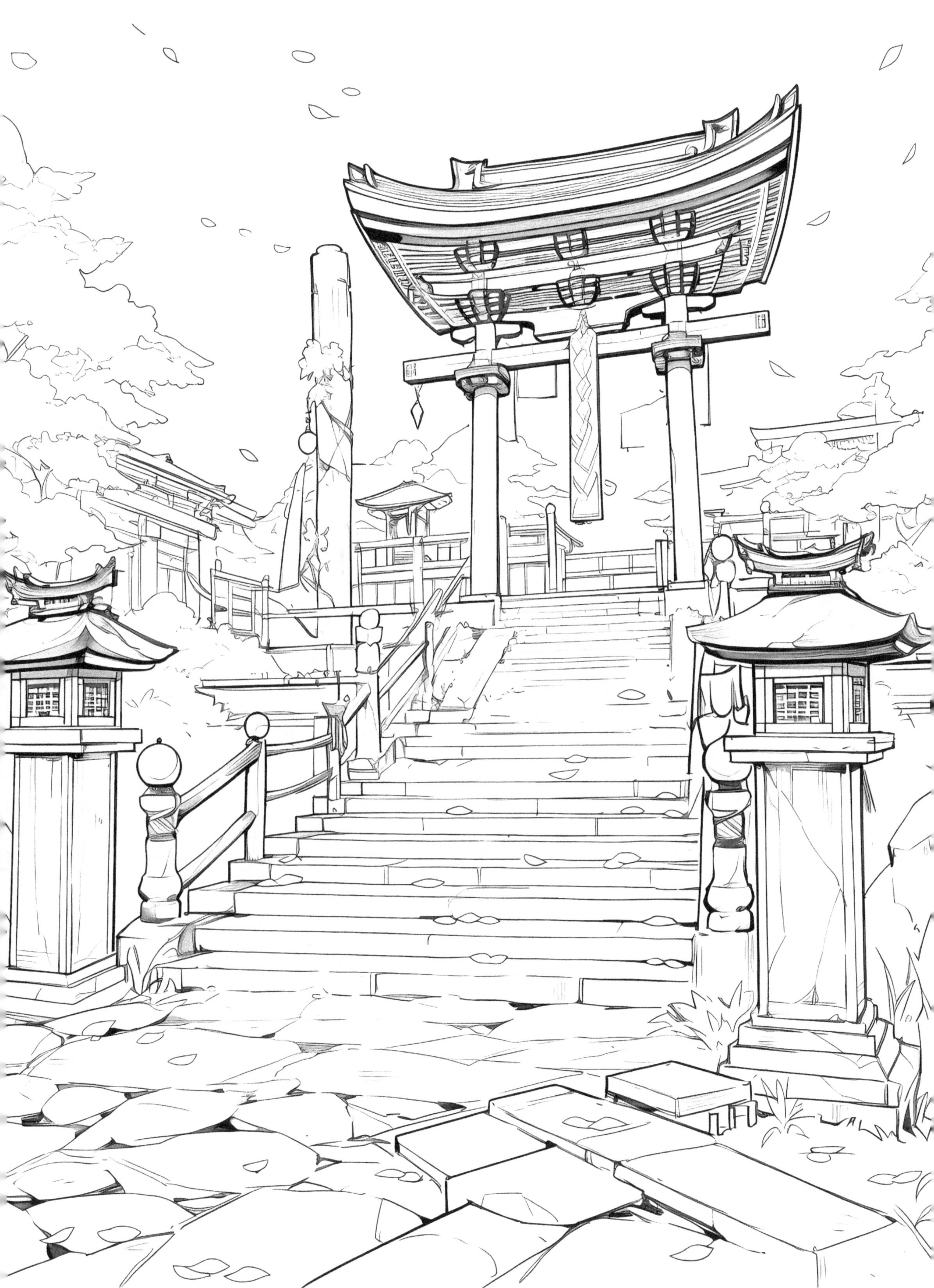

美しい日本の庭園、静寂の楽園

Beautiful Japanese gardens, the
paradise of serenity.

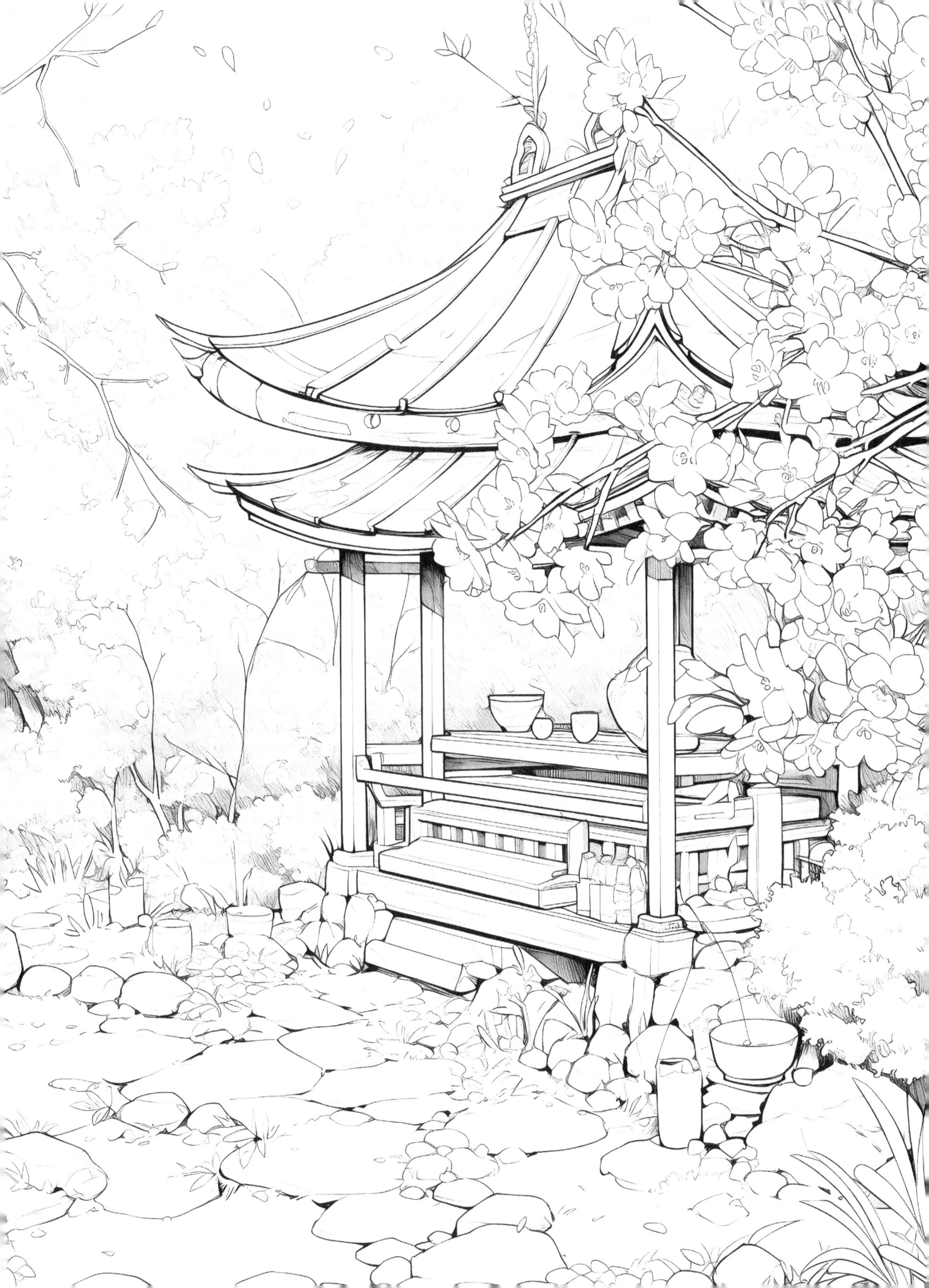

侘び寂び、日本の美意識

Wabi-sabi, the Japanese aesthetic of
beauty in imperfection.

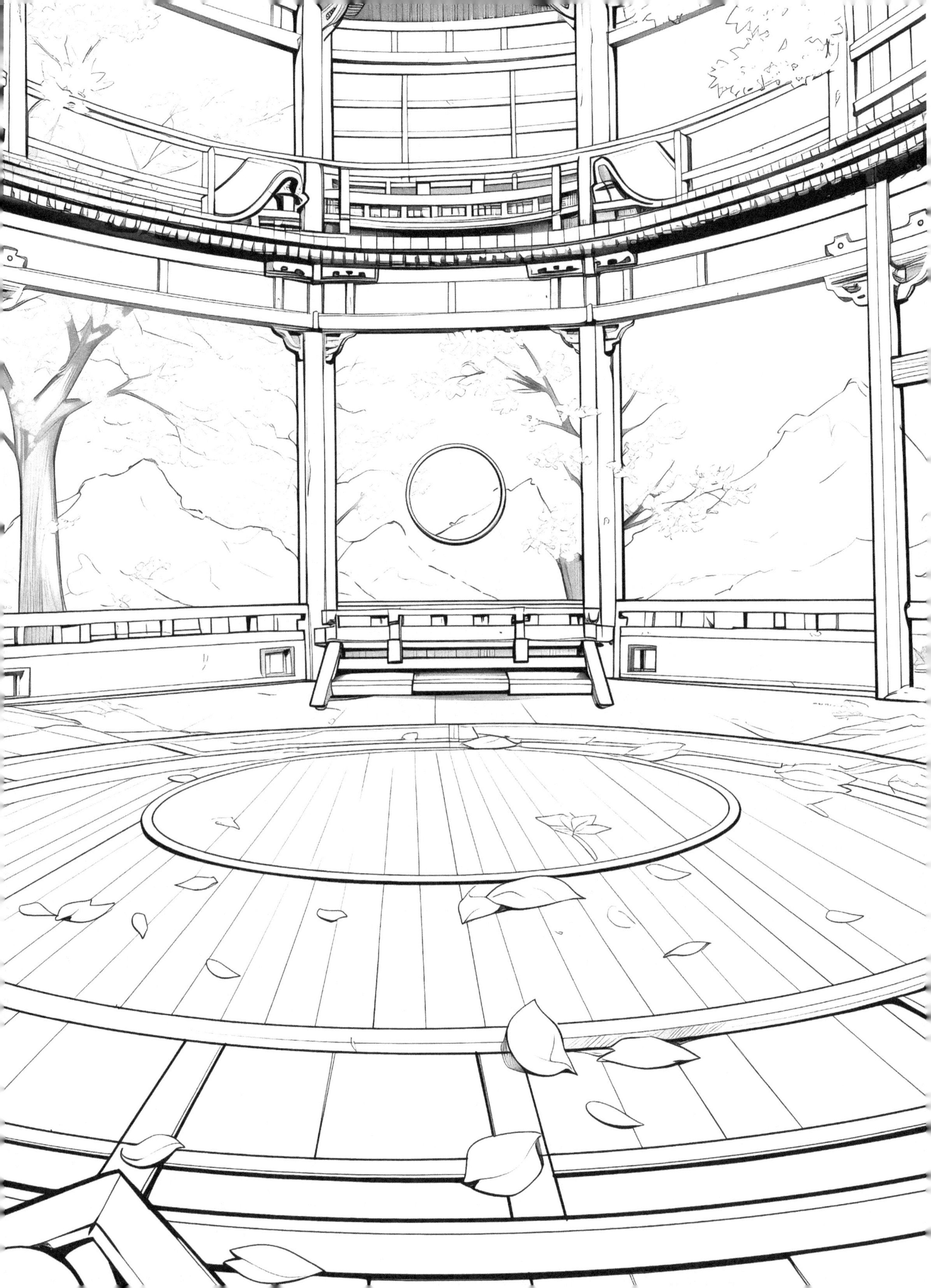

庭は心の鏡

A garden is a mirror of the heart

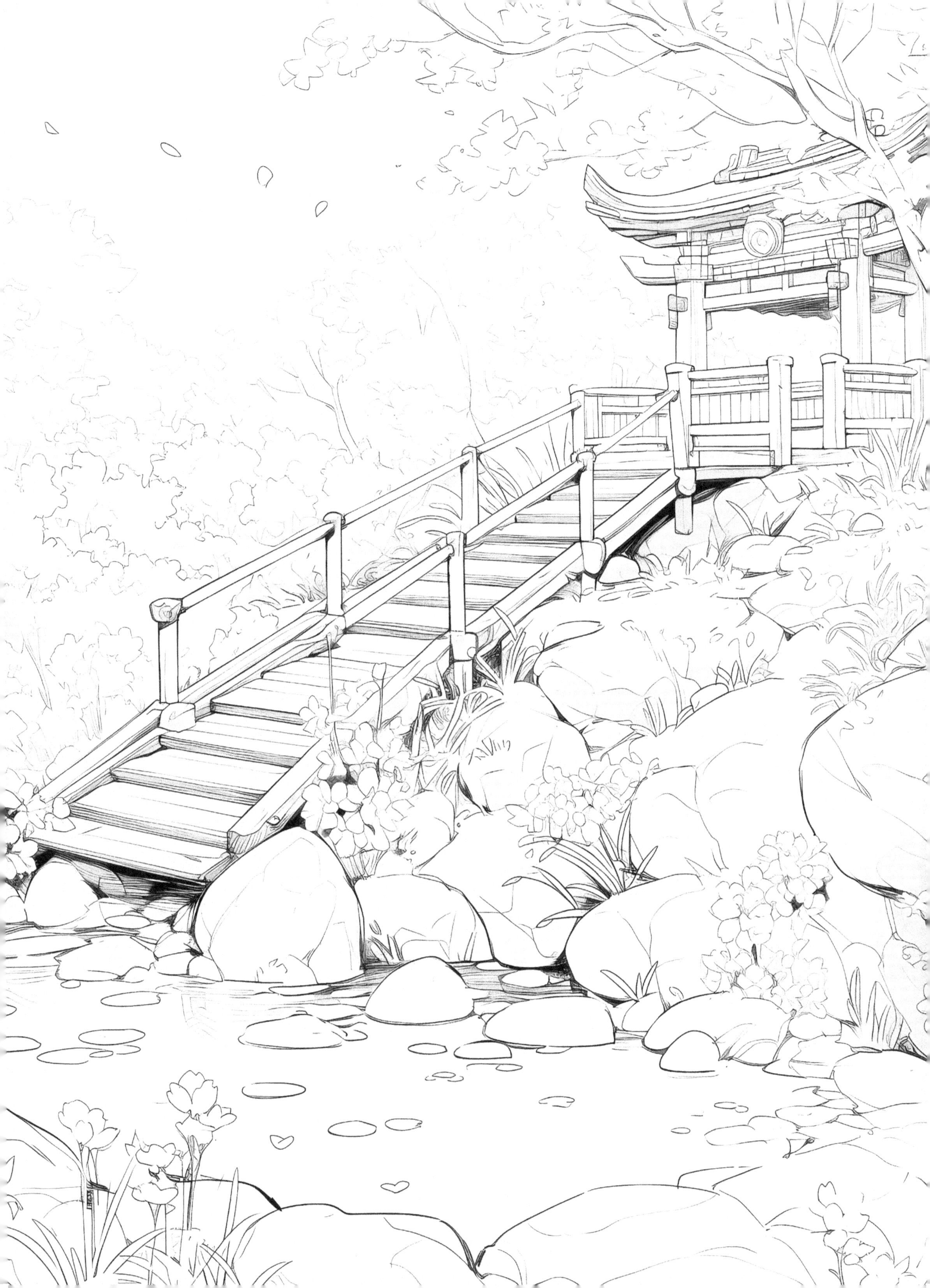

浮かぶ灯り、願いを乗せて

Floating lights, carrying our wishes

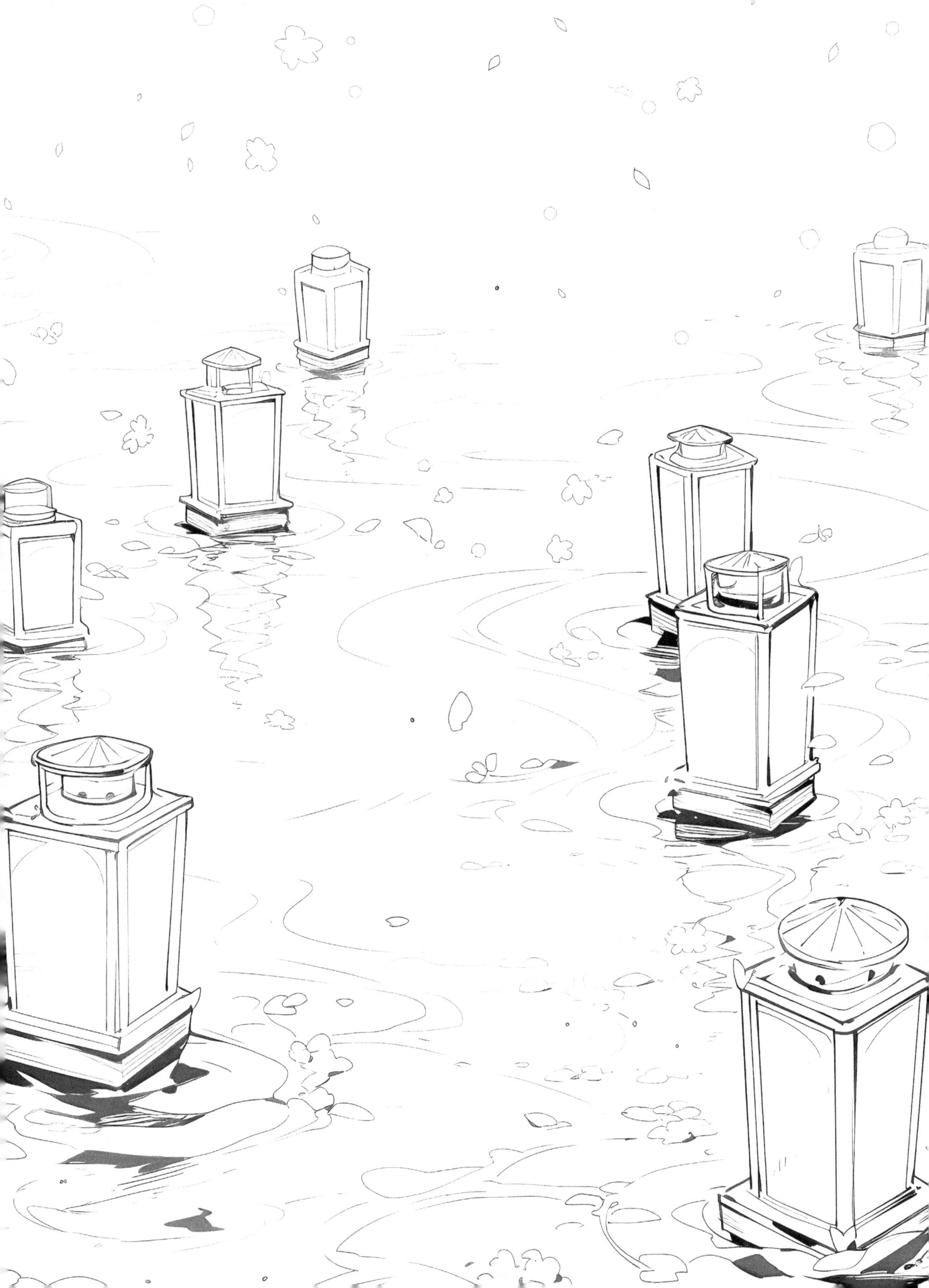

剣術の真髄は道場での厳しい稽古にあり

The essence of swordsmanship lies in
rigorous training at the dojo

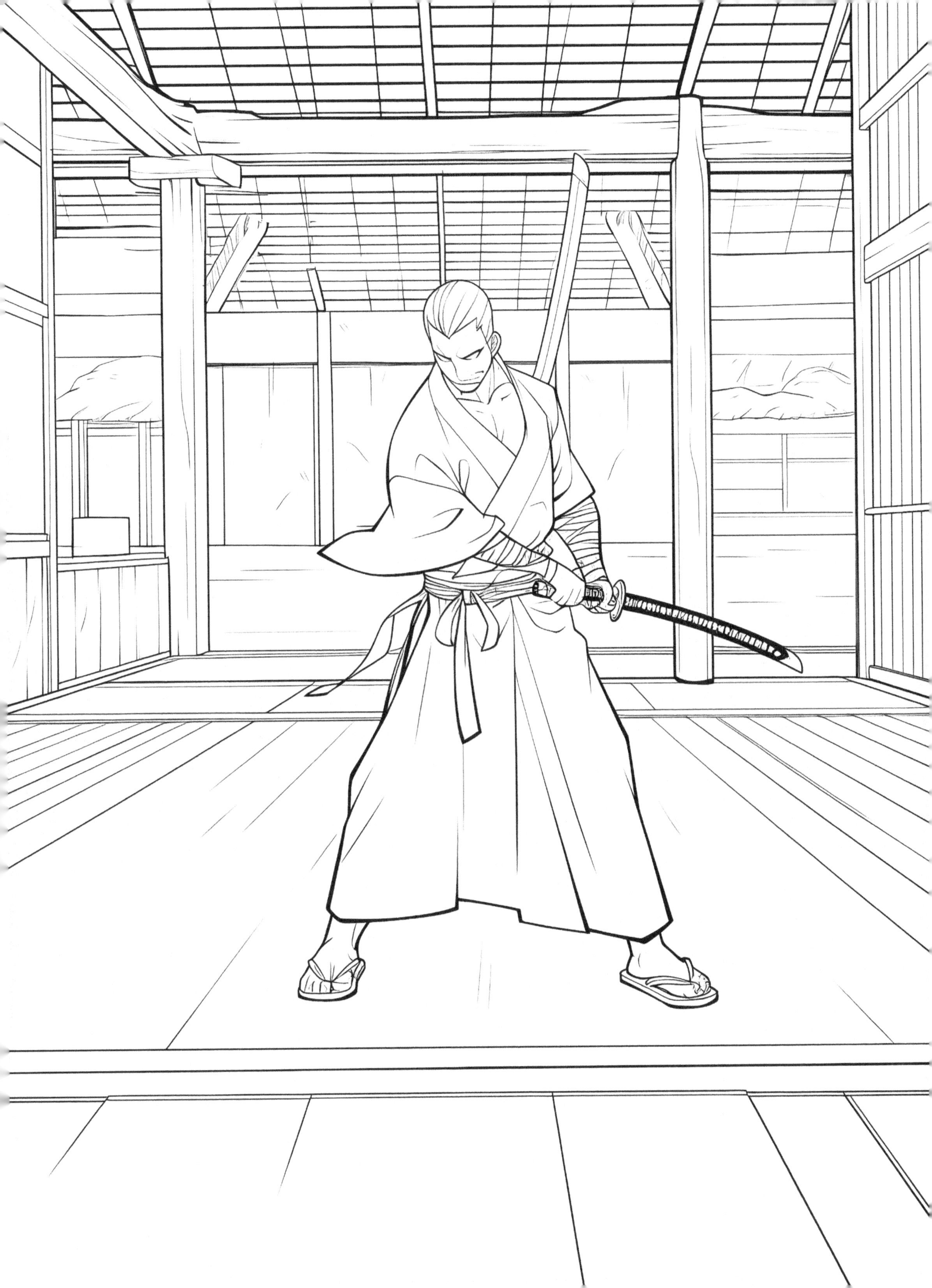

農作業は汗と感謝の表現

Farming is the expression of sweat and
gratitude

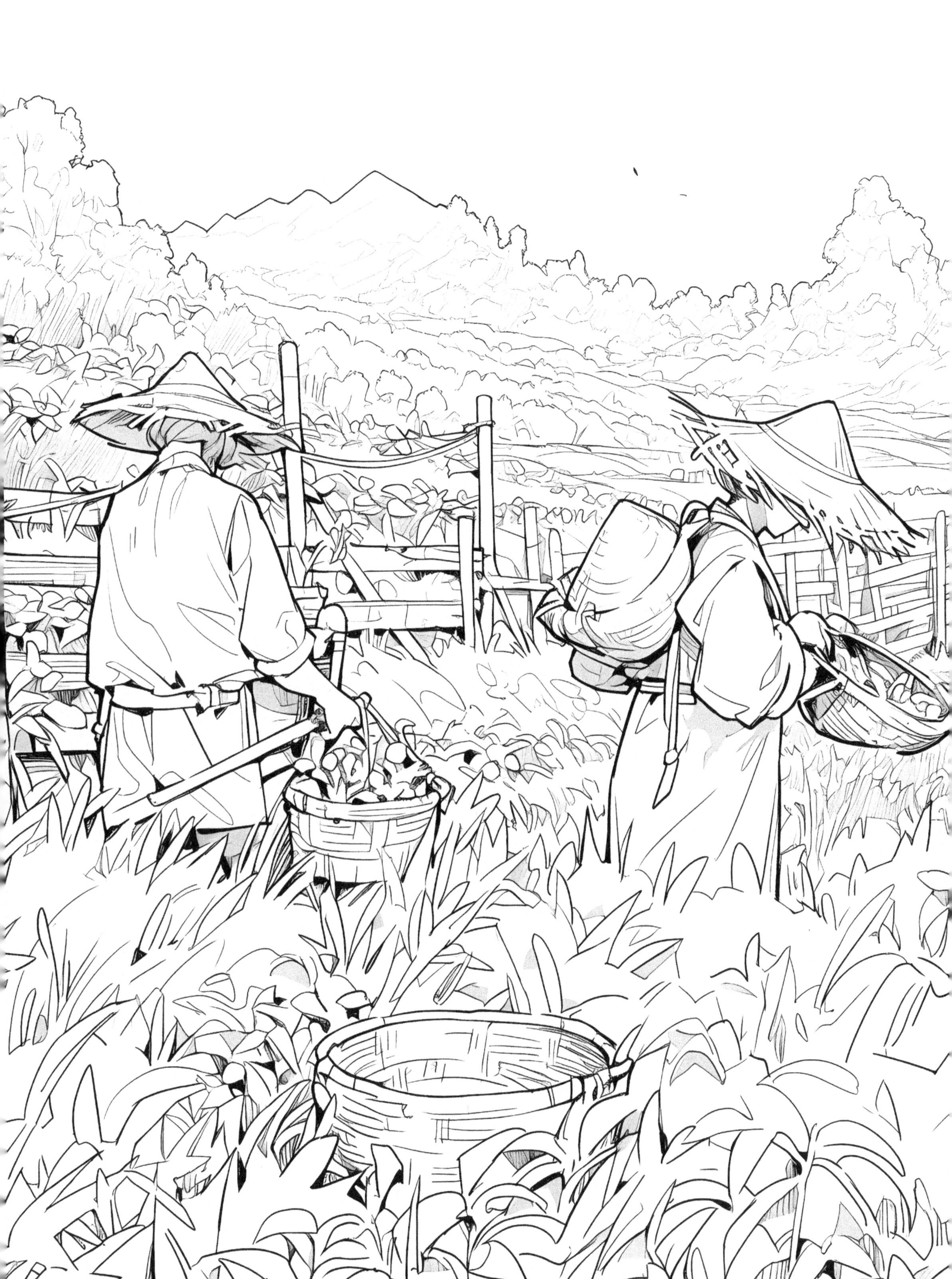

農耕は自然の恵みを謙虚に受け入れること

Farming is humbly accepting the
blessings of nature

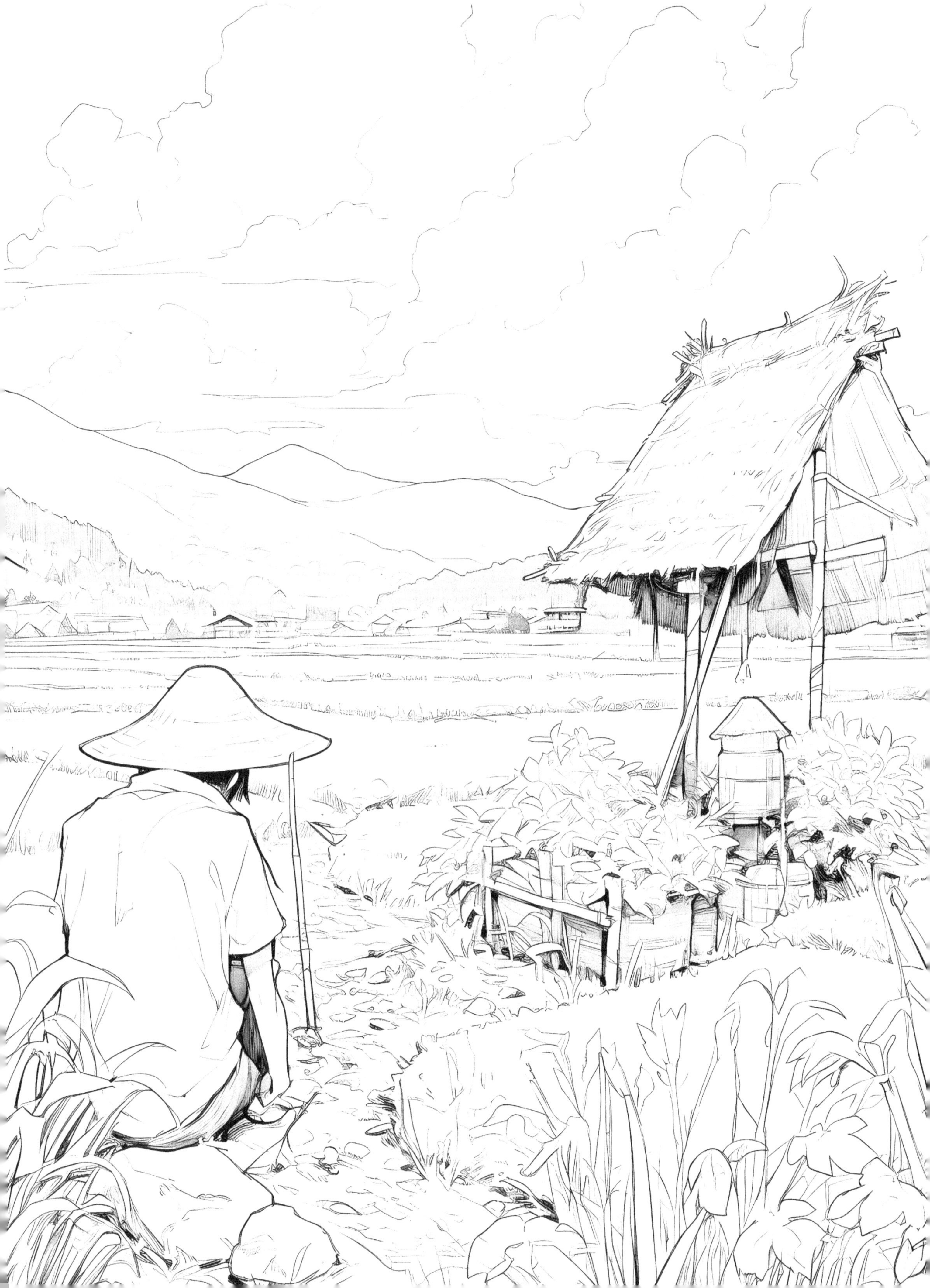

いつもの風景が心に彩りを与える

Everyday scenery adds color to the heart.

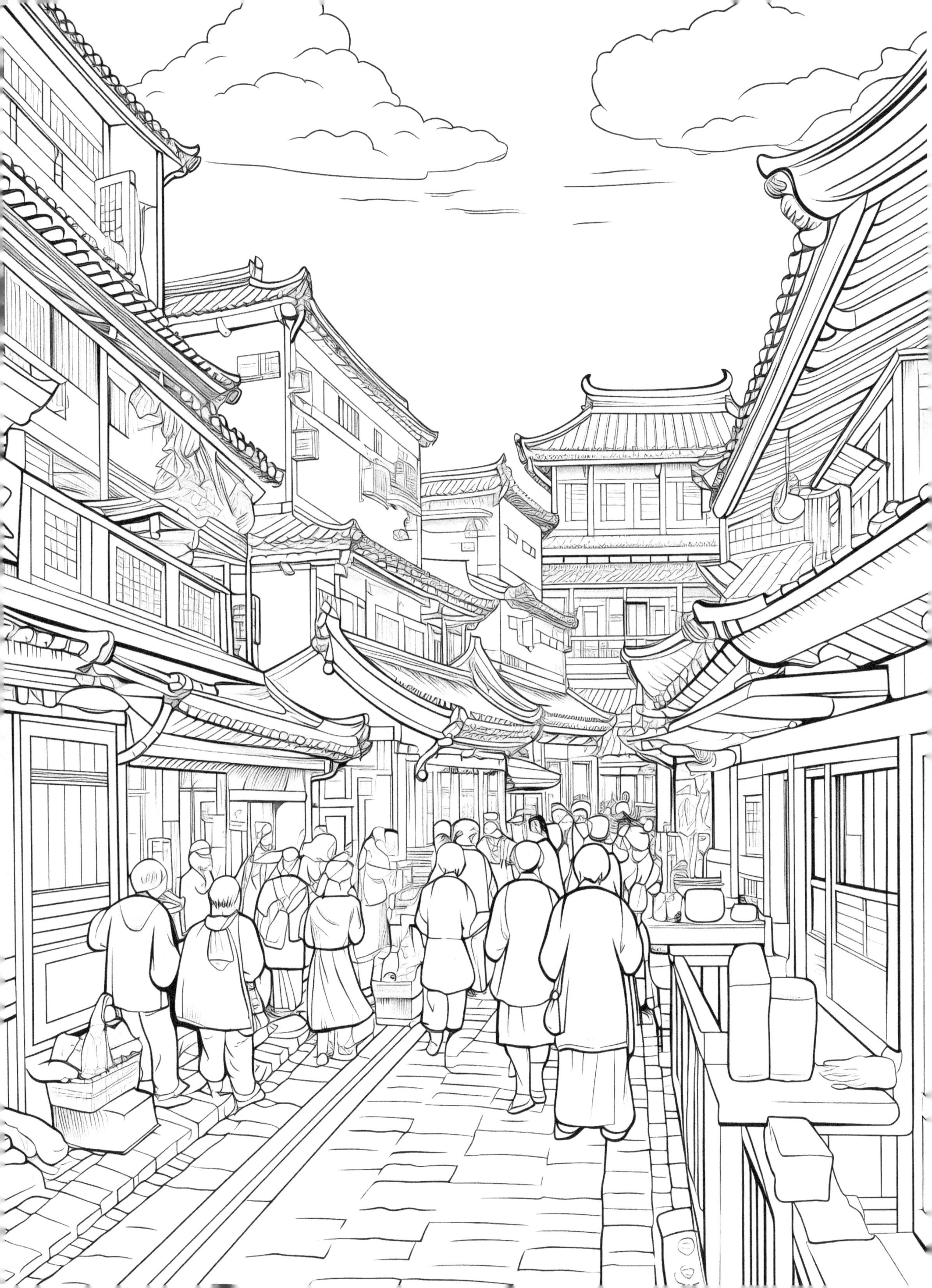

山々の力強さ、心の慰め

The strength of the mountains, solace for
the soul.